field of stars

how many reasons
to follow the Way—
this field of stars

for Kai and Luca
the brightest stars in my universe

field of stars

Lyn Reeves

Walleah Press

© Copyright Lyn Reeves 2019

Published by Walleah Press
PO Box 368
North Hobart
Tasmania 7002 Australia
ralph.wessman@walleahpress.com.au

This book is copyright. Aside from fair dealing for the purpose of study, research, criticism, review, or as otherwise permitted under the Copyright Act, no part may be reproduced by any process without prior written permission. Enquiries should be made to the publisher.

ISBN   978-1-877010-91-0

Text: © Lyn Reeves
Cover design: © Tony Fuery
Cover image: Landscape with Stars, ca 1905-1908, Henri-Edmond Cross (Public Domain).

stirred from dreams—
the chime of a spoon
inside the cup

daybreak
the bay shallows
awash with sky

bush walk. . .
the toddler follows
a line of ants

snow melt
the scent of freesias
opening

in and out of shadow
the winding track
to the mountain top

beginning rain
a soft wind brushes
the casuarinas

in sparse scrub
the honeyeater's wing
flashes yellow

forest clearing
saplings encroach
the abandoned sawmill

broken bridge
a sapling sprouts
from its planks

fern glade
holding green light
in its leaves

rainforest pool
glints of gold
in the orb spider's web

the child shows me
his secret garden—
weeds in flower

quiet garden
listening all day
to leaves

my book forgotten...
the changing script
of clouds

in a strange city
even birdsong speaks
a different tongue

soft rain
beneath the white umbrella
her long black hair

vapour trail
four black kites
circle the day moon

in the park
of a thousand cherry trees
a thousand crows

exchanging gifts—
your sencha
for my leatherwood honey

how quietly sunlight trembles through the bamboo grove

tea arbour
the sound of running water
stills all thoughts

empty bowl
a fragrant liquor
fills it

cobbled lane
a scatter of skinks
on the drystone wall

spinning fleece
her hands enact
an ancient dance

chance meeting
your lined face reveals
how old I've grown

bishops weed in flower. . .
the clack of bobbins
in the lace-maker's hands

old town rivulet
its banks overrun
with forget-me-nots

tattered envelope
the lingering scent
of pressed jasmine

woven into
the blackbird's nest
my shredded poems

old garden
sweet peas entangle
the broken trellis

cloud watching. . .
a high wind
unravels the sky

late spring
the cherry orchard's
tight green fruit

night garden
the magnolia tree
cups moonlight

red sunrise
the bulldozer's engine
revs up

deeper into the forest trees mottled with moss

misted hills
the rasp of a chainsaw
cuts the stillness

felled tree—
bees in the scattered
gum blossom

orphaned joey
tries to climb into
its mother's cold pouch

deepening the quiet
murmur of wind
through the she-oak grove

ablaze with purple – the samphire flats in flower

zebra-striped dragonfly
helicopters
across the swamp

tranquil water
black against the reeds
duck-shooter hides

somewhere
among these reeds
a bittern's secret nest

gentle breeze
strumming light
through grass-tree leaves

burgeoning moon
how close the sky
above the casuarinas

spider web
balanced on waterweeds
radiates moonlight

on the patio
possum prints
in apricot juice

thud on my window
the blackbird flies off
on unsteady wings

sunrise. . .
an amber glow
fills the glass teapot

in the boiling kettle
a rumble
of distant waves

summer beach
the sea wind sings
through my bones

sea haze
the tang of salt
on my skin

on white sand
a cluster of bluebottles
dries to indigo

summer breeze
the blue
of everything

afternoon beach
the young lovers cast
a single shadow

distant thunder
silently over the ocean
rain

rescue launch
searching for the drowned man
in all that water

the silence
      between waves
breaking

      heavy rain. . .
      the blood-red peony
      spills its petals

falling leaf
light spirals
to earth

blue-tongued lizard
pretending to be
blue gum leaves

on the lawn
four striped deck chairs
taking the sun

sunbaking
the dog beside me
on his back

bamboo blinds
cutting sunlight
into stripes

the dead spider
on the bamboo blind
has moved

rain-soaked trees
the liquid warble
of bush birds

summer lake
a feather drifts
on clouds

tourist track
laughter
in ten languages

shutter-click
the waterfall
flows again

through misted trees
the bush hut's
chimney smoke

afternoon storm
the wine glass fills
with rain

mother's best china
left to me
still unused

garage sale
the cracked china teapot's
tannin scent

tea and scones
the heirloom milk jug's
family secrets

lowering sun—
caught in its glow
a lacework of leaves

country dance
the tea urn
runs hot

campfire embers
stars shine out
from the blackened billy

moon shimmer
a ringtail possum
scales the banksia tree

plastic playground
my kids climb into
the pepper tree

long day's dusk. . .
in quietness now
the carousel horses

among briars
all along the roadside
crimson rosehips

blackberry season
a soft blue haze
on the hills

roadside flower stall
no change
for the honesty box

underground platform
a cool wind
precedes the train

underground car park
behind a wire grille
the rock art of street kids

wildlife park
the echidna
paces its cage

fog bound city
the blackbird's feet and beak
bright yellow

crowded mall
a stranger's hand
touches mine

symphony concert
only the conductor
allowed to dance

junk shop. . .
cobwebs curtain
the dollhouse windows

April gale
the carp windsock
tugs at its hook

the softness
a feather's silent fall
onto rock

heavy skies
the uncertain shapes
of shadow and light

afternoon light
grandfather dances
in a shower of leaves

that distant ridge
I'll never climb. . .
autumn rain

icy wind
the old post and rail
speckled with lichen

approaching night
the river echoes
the sky's depths

the *Last Post*. . .
only two poppies
on his coffin

overcast sky
the light
from a single dandelion

from laden branches
one by one
ripe plums fall

                        worn stone steps
                        curve upwards
                        into green shadow

how fragile
this viewing platform
above the deep ravine

mountain fog lifts
and the river streams
in and out of view

fractured coast
headlands repeat
into haze

beyond the ranges
deep in fog
a clear horizon

clear river
a school of bream
shadows the shallows

winter blue—
the quiet bay
erupts with dolphins

in the shallows
of the dark river
light ripples

winter creek
a rumour
of platypus

days close in
this morning the valley
lies deeper in mist

removing the rings
from my dead mother's hands
the nurse speaks gently

against grey
a solitary tree
bent to the shape of the gale

hollow eucalypt the forest quiet fills it

chill morning
a beach of pebbles
only the waves pick up

softening
the rock face
evening shadows

rose garden
the neat-edged beds
of straggly blooms

in a rose garden
far from here
my mother's ashes

dark pines
the cemetery angel's
broken wing

clearing skies
open-faced on the wet grass
a red camellia

goodbye hug
her scent on my jacket
all the way home

lone fisherman
casts out
on a lake of mist

wind-ruffled sea
white and black clouds
share the sky

storm coming
the green shallows
darken

outgoing tide
the shell of a dinghy
half-buried in sand

twilight. . .
winter branches fill
with birdsong

sound of the bell. . .
listening in silence
for the silence

campfire smoke. . .
conversations drift
into a dusk of stars

Lyn Reeves writes poetry, haiku and short fiction. She is co-editor of *Echidna Tracks: Australian Haiku* and Vice President of The Australian Haiku Society. From 1994-2012, she edited the haiku section of the literary journal, *Famous Reporter*, and has guest edited for numerous haiku journals. Her first haiku collection, *Walking the Tideline*, (2001) is now available as a free e-book download from The Haiku Foundation Digital Library.

Lyn's work has earned grants from Arts Tasmania and the Australia Council. She has been a featured reader at several writers' festivals and collaborated with painters, printmakers, musicians, photographers, mountain workers and scientists for various exhibitions and poetry events. Her poetry has been translated into French and Russian, set to music by composer Rosemary Austen and read on ABC Poetica. She lives in Hobart, where she co-convenes the haiku group, Watersmeet.

Thanks

Field of Stars brings together many of my haiku that have been published since my first collection, *Walking the Tideline*, appeared in 2001. My appreciation goes to those who have helped bring this book into being: to Ralph Wessman for including it in his fine list of poetry titles and for his patience in waiting for the completed manuscript; to Ron Moss and Jane Williams for reading and feedback on early drafts; to Hayley Reeves for technical help and her keen eye; and to all the members of Watersmeet for their support and friendship. I am indebted to Tony Fuery for his cover design and also to Simon Hanson and Ron Moss for their generous endorsements. I am also grateful to Fullers Bookshop for a Café Poet residency in 2013, where I first began to compile this collection, and to Pete Hay, Dick Bett Gallery and the Tasmanian Land Conservancy for the Poets & Painters retreat at the Big Punchbowl, Freycinet, in 2016. Finally, I owe my deep appreciation to my partner, Andrew, for his support and for his companionship along the Way where many of these haiku were found.

Acknowledgements

I thank the editors of the following journals and anthologies where most of the haiku in this collection have appeared:

All the Way Home: Aging in Haiku (ed. Robert Epstein), Middle Island Press, 2019; *The Attitude of Cups*, Melbourne Poets Union, 2011; Australian Haiku Society: Haiku Strings; *Blue Giraffe*; *Celebrating the Big Punchbowl: poets and painters*, Tasmanian Land Conservancy & Dick Bett Gallery, 2017; *clear water: the paper wasp jack stamm haiku anthology 2004*; *Darkness*, Per Diem Archive, The Haiku Foundation, 2019; *The Dreaming Collection*; *Echidna Tracks: Australian Haiku*; *Evening Breeze: the anthology from the inaugural Janice M. Bostok award*, Paper Wasp, 2012; *Famous Reporter*; *Going Down Swinging*; *The Haiku Calendar 2015 & 2018*, Snapshot Press; *Haiku Windows*, The Haiku Foundation, 2018; *FreeXpression*; *the infinity we swim in*, NZPS, 2007; *the ink brushed distance*, Lyn Reeves, Walleah Press, 2008; *Kokako*; *moments in the whirlwind*, NZPS, 2009; *Butterfly Dream*, Neverending Story; *Notes from the Gean*; *paper wasp*; *Poam* (Melbourne Poets Union); *Poems to wear: from Japan and Australia*, Ginninderra Press, 2016; *Second Australian Haiku Anthology*, 2006; *Small Worlds / paintings by Luke Wagner, words by Lyn Reeves*, 2017; *Presence*; *Still heading out: an anthology of Australian and New Zealand haiku*, 2013; *Stylus Poetry Journal*; *Third Australian Haiku Anthology* 2011; *Tug of the current: The Red Moon anthology of English-language haiku 2004*, Red Moon Press, 2005; *Watersmeet: haiku*, 2005; *Windfall: Australian haiku*; *World Haiku Review*; *Yellow Moon*.

By the same author

Collections

Walking the Tideline (Pardalote Press, 2001)
Speaking with Ghosts (Ginninderra Press, 2002)
Beads (Picaro Press, 2007)
The ink brushed distance (Walleah Press, 2008)
Designs on the Body (Interactive Press, 2011)
Small Worlds with artist Luke Wagner, 2017

Anthologies

Republican Dreaming: 5 poets (Bumble-bee Books, 1999)
Moorilla Mosaic: contemporary Tasmanian writing (Bumble-bee Books, 2001)
Watersmeet: haiku (Pardalote Press, 2005)
Seasoned with Honey: a four-poet anthology (Walleah Press, 2008)
Celebrating the Big Punchbowl: Poets and Painters, Tasmanian Land Conservancy & Dick Bett Gallery, 2017

Audio

Designs on the Body, CD, Drums Records, 2017

www.ingramcontent.com/pod-product-compliance
Lightning Source LLC
Chambersburg PA
CBHW021129080526
44587CB00012B/1193